HODDER HOME LEARNING

# Mental Arithmetic

AGE



Dr Bill Gillham

Illustrated by Sascha Lipscomb

Mental arithmetic is sometimes neglected in primary education; not all children know how to work out sums in their heads.

There are three sections in this book: **Addition and subtraction**, **Multiplication and division** and **Mental arithmetic in real life**. Each finishes with a short test. There are also five speed training exercises. Speed is important in mental arithmetic; practice with *easy* sums is the way to achieve it.

## How to help your child

- Keep sessions short and regular; one or two pages a day is ideal.
- Children – and adults – easily get anxious about mathematics, so take a relaxed attitude to any difficulties.
- In the speed tests, emphasise to your child that they should work at their own pace – and improve on that.
- Read the notes on page 2 together, and make sure your child knows what to do on each page (especially where 'short-cut' strategies are given).
- Mental arithmetic is a skill we use every day. Try to give your child regular, real-life practice.
- Focus on your child's successes, but if they make a mistake, explain where they have gone wrong.

*Hodder Children's Books*

NATIONAL CONFEDERATION OF PARENT TEACHER ASSOCIATIONS

**The only home learning programme supported by the NCPTA**

# What is mental arithmetic?

**Mental arithmetic is arithmetic in which you do the working out...**

**...not on paper...**

**...not on a calculator...**

**...not on a computer...**

**...but in your head!**

# Why is it useful?

- **You don't always have a calculator handy.**
- **It's often faster to do a sum in your head.**
- **If you can do simple sums quickly in your head, it will help you to do BIG sums.**
- **If you can't do simple sums in your head, you won't be able to understand calculator work with bigger numbers. Calculators are best for big numbers.**

**cm** means **centimetres**
**m** means **metres**
**km** means **kilometres**

**g** means **grams**
**kg** means **kilograms**

**100 centimetres = 1 metre**
**1000 metres = 1 kilometre**

**1000 grams = 1 kilogram**

# ‹‹‹‹ Speed training 1 ››››

Here are four speed tests.
Write the answers in the boxes.
Time yourself for each test.

## ‹ Speed Test 1 ›

| | | |
|---|---|---|
| 1 | 1 + 2 = | |
| 2 | 4 ÷ 2 = | |
| 3 | 1 x 3 = | |
| 4 | 2 – 1 = | |
| 5 | 5 – 3 = | |
| 6 | 2 x 2 = | |
| 7 | 6 ÷ 3 = | |
| 8 | 5 + 1 = | |

**Time** ☐ **seconds**

## ‹ Speed Test 2 ›

| | | |
|---|---|---|
| 1 | 3 ÷ 1 = | |
| 2 | 6 + 2 = | |
| 3 | 4 + 4 = | |
| 4 | 10 ÷ 5 = | |
| 5 | 1 x 10 = | |
| 6 | 7 – 3 = | |
| 7 | 10 ÷ 10 = | |
| 8 | 2 x 5 = | |

**Time** ☐ **seconds**

## ‹ Speed Test 3 ›

| | | |
|---|---|---|
| 1 | 6 + 4 = | |
| 2 | 1 – 1 = | |
| 3 | 6 ÷ 2 = | |
| 4 | 3 x 3 = | |
| 5 | 4 x 2 = | |
| 6 | 9 + 1 = | |
| 7 | 2 x 1 = | |
| 8 | 8 ÷ 2 = | |

**Time** ☐ **seconds**

## ‹ Speed Test 4 ›

| | | |
|---|---|---|
| 1 | 6 – 0 = | |
| 2 | 5 x 2 = | |
| 3 | 7 ÷ 1 = | |
| 4 | 7 + 3 = | |
| 5 | 0 + 0 = | |
| 6 | 9 – 3 = | |
| 7 | 5 + 5 = | |
| 8 | 10 ÷ 2 = | |

**Time** ☐ **seconds**

**Best time with all answers correct**

☐ **seconds**

# Addition and subtraction

## Mental magic (addition)

**37 + 25 = ?**

**Add the tens first.**

**30 + 20 = 50**

**Then add the units.**

**7 + 5 = 12**

**Then add the two together.**

**50 + 12 = 62**

Now try these:

1. 25 + 36 = ☐
2. 17 + 24 = ☐
3. 37 + 25 = ☐
4. 48 + 14 = ☐
5. 27 + 25 = ☐
6. 58 + 13 = ☐
7. 48 + 44 = ☐
8. 37 + 35 = ☐
9. 78 + 14 = ☐
10. 67 + 15 = ☐

Score 2 points for each correct answer.

TOTAL ☐ / 20

# Mental magic (subtraction)

**35 – 16 = ?**

**Take away the tens first.**

**35 – 10 = 25**

**Then take away the units.**

**25 – 6 = 19**

Now try these:

1. **23 – 14 =** ☐
2. **33 – 14 =** ☐
3. **53 – 14 =** ☐
4. **45 – 27 =** ☐
5. **56 – 38 =** ☐
6. **27 – 16 =** ☐
7. **30 – 11 =** ☐
8. **33 – 15 =** ☐
9. **36 – 18 =** ☐
10. **45 – 17 =** ☐

Score 2 points for each correct answer.

**SCORE** /20

# Words into sums (addition and subtraction)

**10 − 2 = 8**

**You have twelve Chocobars and you give four of them away. How many do you have left?**

**Read the question carefully, and ask yourself two questions:**

**1 What is the sign?**
**Is it: addition +**
**or subtraction? −**

**2 What are the numbers?**

**The sum is: 12 − 4 = 8**

# Practice page

**1** **You've saved £14.00 towards your holiday and your mother gives you an extra £6.00. How much do you have now?**

| Number | Sign | Number | | Answer |
|---|---|---|---|---|
| | | | = | |

SCORE /4

**2** **If your football team has scored seventeen goals this season and scores four in today's match, how many goals is that altogether?**

| Number | Sign | Number | | Answer |
|---|---|---|---|---|
| | | | = | |

SCORE /4

**3** **If there are twenty-eight children in your class and four are away with flu, how many are in class?**

| Number | Sign | Number | | Answer |
|---|---|---|---|---|
| | | | = | |

SCORE /4

**4** **If you've bought twelve tins of dinosaur food and your pet dinosaur's eaten ten, how many are left?**

| Number | Sign | Number | | Answer |
|---|---|---|---|---|
| | | | = | |

SCORE /4

**5** **You have 31p in coins but you lose 15p. How much do you have left?**

| Number | Sign | Number | | Answer |
|---|---|---|---|---|
| | | | = | |

SCORE /4

TOTAL /20

This page has allowed you to do some working out with pencil and paper. From now on, you do all the working out in your head!

# TEST 1

✗ or ✓

1. If you have 50p and you spend 10p, how much do you have left?
2. What are one, two, three and four altogether?
3. In a burger-eating competition your sister eats twenty-one burgers. You eat four fewer than she does. How many do you manage to eat?
4. Your little brother was 90cm tall last year but he's grown another 10cm. How tall is he now?
5. If you had £3.00 and you've spent half of it on a magazine, how much do you have left?
6. You do twelve sums, but four of them are wrong. How many do you get right?
7. This sum has the wrong answer: 17 + 14 = 35. What is the right answer?
8. What are ten, twenty and thirty altogether?
9. You weigh 30kg. If your friend weighs 3kg less than you, how much does she weigh?
10. Your sister is 1m 45cm tall. You are 1m 25cm tall. How much taller than you is she?

Score 2 points for each correct answer.

TOTAL
/20

# Speed training 2

Remember to time yourself for each test.

## Speed Test 1

1. 2 x 2 =
2. 5 – 1 =
3. 7 + 3 =
4. 6 ÷ 2 =
5. 3 x 3 =
6. 10 – 9 =
7. 2 + 7 =
8. 9 ÷ 3 =

**Time** ☐ **seconds**

## Speed Test 2

1. 6 + 4 =
2. 10 + 1 =
3. 4 ÷ 4 =
4. 10 – 10 =
5. 2 x 4 =
6. 9 – 8 =
7. 1 x 1 =
8. 8 ÷ 4 =

**Time** ☐ **seconds**

## Speed Test 3

1. 6 + 2 =
2. 10 – 3 =
3. 10 ÷ 5 =
4. 2 x 6 =
5. 5 x 3 =
6. 9 ÷ 3 =
7. 2 + 1 =
8. 9 – 9 =

**Time** ☐ **seconds**

## Speed Test 4

1. 10 ÷ 2 =
2. 2 x 1 =
3. 5 + 4 =
4. 4 ÷ 2 =
5. 6 + 3 =
6. 10 – 9 =
7. 2 x 5 =
8. 10 – 7 =

**Time** ☐ **seconds**

**Best time with all answers correct**

☐ **seconds**

# Multiplication and division

## Mental magic (multiplication)

**3 x 26 = ?**

**Multiply the tens first.**

**3 x 20 = 60**

**Then multiply the units.**

**3 x 6 = 18**

**Then add the two together.**

**60 + 18 = 78**

---

Now try these:

1. 3 x 22 =
2. 4 x 15 =
3. 5 x 13 =
4. 3 x 16 =
5. 2 x 24 =
6. 3 x 25 =
7. 3 x 18 =
8. 4 x 21 =
9. 2 x 27 =
10. 6 x 14 =

Score 2 points for each correct answer.

TOTAL /20

# Handy hints with tables

| | |
|---|---|
| **2 x** | • **The answer always ends in 2, 4, 6, 8 or 0.** |
| **3 x** | • **You can "double up" to make the 6 x table.**<br>**7 x 6 = ?** **7 x 3 = 21 Double 21 → 42** **7 x 6 = 42** |
| **4 x** | • **You can "double up" to make the 8 x table.**<br>**9 x 8 = ?** **9 x 4 = 36 Double 36 → 72** **9 x 8 = 72** |
| **5 x** | • **The answer always ends in 5 or 0.** |
| **6 x** | • **You can "double up" to make the 12 x table.**<br>**6 x 12 = ?** **6 x 6 = 36 Double 36 → 72** **6 x 12 = 72** |
| **7 x** | • **This is a hard one like the 9x table. Try going forwards or backwards.**<br>**9 x 7 = ?** **10 x 7 = 70 Take away 7 → 63** **9 x 7 = 63** |
| **8 x** | • **The answer always ends in 2, 4, 6, 8 or 0.** |
| **9 x** | • **The digits in the answer always add up to 9.**<br>**5 x 9 = 45** **4 + 5 = 9** **7 x 9 = 63** **6 + 3 = 9**<br>• **9 x 9 = ?** **10 x 9 = 90 Take away 9 → 81** **9 x 9 = 81** |
| **10 x** | • **This is an easy one! Just put 0 after the number you are multiplying by.** **5 x 10 = ?** **5 0 → 50** **5 x 10 = 50** |
| **11 x** | • **This is easy... up to 10 x 11.**<br>• **11 x 11 = ?** **Add 11 to 10 x 11 (110)** **11 x 11 = 121**<br>• **12 x 11 = ?** **Add 11 to 11 x 11 (121)** **12 x 11 = 132** |
| **12 x** | • **5 x 12 and 10 x 12 are easy; you can go forwards or backwards to get the answers next to these.**<br>**9 x 12 = ?** **10 x 12 = 120**<br>**Take away 12.** **9 x 12 = 108** |

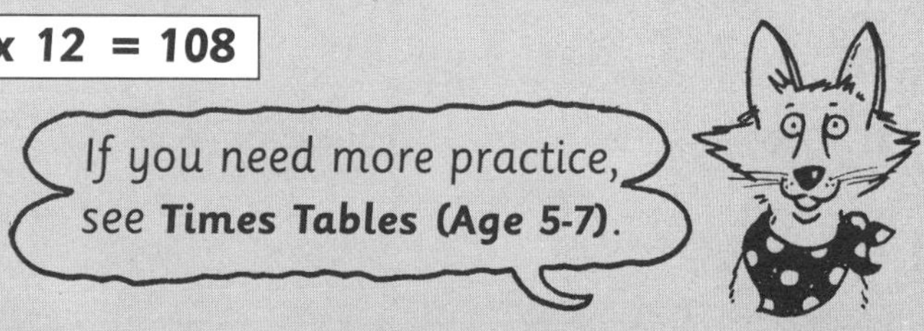

## Table Test 1

1. 6 x 6 =
2. 3 x 7 =
3. 9 x 11 =
4. 2 x 12 =
5. 9 x 8 =
6. 6 x 12 =
7. 11 x 10 =
8. 7 x 6 =
9. 7 x 5 =
10. 4 x 4 =

TOTAL /10

## Table Test 2

1. 7 x 3 =
2. 10 x 10 =
3. 5 x 7 =
4. 5 x 12 =
5. 4 x 6 =
6. 4 x 12 =
7. 7 x 11 =
8. 12 x 12 =
9. 9 x 7 =
10. 7 x 9 =

TOTAL /10

## Table Test 3

1. 9 x 2 =
2. 10 x 9 =
3. 8 x 6 =
4. 3 x 12 =
5. 4 x 7 =
6. 11 x 11 =
7. 11 x 9 =
8. 5 x 8 =
9. 8 x 9 =
10. 6 x 6 =

TOTAL /10

## Table Test 4

1. 7 x 4 =
2. 8 x 8 =
3. 5 x 9 =
4. 6 x 11 =
5. 11 x 12 =
6. 6 x 9 =
7. 7 x 12 =
8. 9 x 8 =
9. 10 x 11 =
10. 12 x 9 =

TOTAL /10

# Words into sums (multiplication)

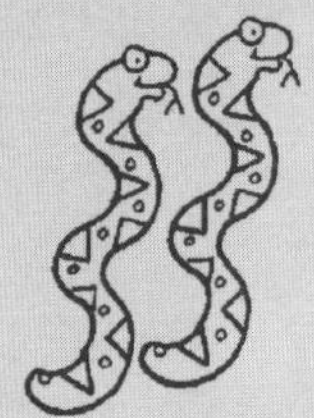

**Ten children get two snakes each.
How many do they get altogether?**

**You can solve this problem in two ways:**

**1** **There are 10 sets of 2 snakes. As there is the same number in each set, you can multiply...**

**10 x 2 = 20**

**... or you can add.**

**2** **2 + 2 + 2 + 2 + 2 + 2 + 2 + 2 + 2 + 2 = 20**

**There are three children. One gets six snakes,
one gets four and one gets two.
How many snakes do they get altogether?**

**You can't multiply here, because each set contains a different number of snakes.**

**You have to add: 6 + 4 + 2 = 12**

# Mental magic (division)

**72 ÷ 6 = ?**

Now try these:

1. **40 ÷ 5 =** ☐
2. **28 ÷ 7 =** ☐
3. **60 ÷ 10 =** ☐
4. **24 ÷ 8 =** ☐
5. **20 ÷ 5 =** ☐
6. **55 ÷ 11 =** ☐
7. **45 ÷ 9 =** ☐
8. **36 ÷ 12 =** ☐
9. **100 ÷ 10 =** ☐
10. **27 ÷ 3 =** ☐

11. **22 ÷ 5 =** ☐ **r** ☐
12. **16 ÷ 3 =** ☐ **r** ☐
13. **22 ÷ 3 =** ☐ **r** ☐
14. **26 ÷ 8 =** ☐ **r** ☐
15. **50 ÷ 7 =** ☐ **r** ☐

Score 2 points for each correct answer.

| TOTAL |
|---|
| /30 |

# Words into sums (division)

**share** **each** **average** **everyone**

**You've scored sixty runs for your cricket team in five matches.**
**What's your average?**

**This is a division sum.**

**60 ÷ 5 = 12**

**£10.00 is shared amongst five children.**
**How much do they get each?**

**This is a division sum too.**

**£10 ÷ 5 = £2.00**

**You were given twenty-four presents at your birthday party.**
**Everyone gave you two presents.**
**How many people came to your party?**

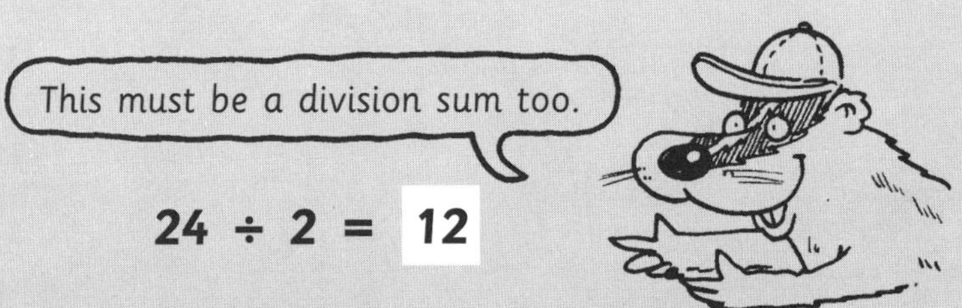


**24 ÷ 2 = 12**

# Mental magic (multiplication)

**20 x 1 000 000 = ?**

**Multiply:**

**2 x 1 = 2**

**Then count the noughts in <u>both</u> numbers.**

**Write the seven noughts after the 2.**

**20 000 000**

**Remember that you only multiply the figures.**

Now try these:

1. 6 x 30 =
2. 30 x 60 =
3. 10 x 100 =
4. 5 x 2 000 =
5. 12 x 2 000 =
6. 3 x 10 000 =
7. 4 x 20 000 =
8. 2 x 1 000 000 =
9. 4 x 2 000 000 =
10. 30 x 3 000 000 =

Score 2 points for each correct answer.

TOTAL
20

# Practice page

**1 If a vampire eats two tins of bat food a day, how many tins does he need for a week?**

| Number | Sign | Number | | Answer |
|---|---|---|---|---|
| | | | = | |

Score 1 point for each correctly completed box.

SCORE /4

**2 If there are three computers in a class of twenty-four children, how many children share each computer?**

| Number | Sign | Number | | Answer |
|---|---|---|---|---|
| | | | = | |

SCORE /4

**3 If six children each buy three comics, how many do they have altogether?**

| Number | Sign | Number | | Answer |
|---|---|---|---|---|
| | | | = | |

SCORE /4

**4 If sheep wore shoes, how many shoes would you need for six sheep?**

| Number | Sign | Number | | Answer |
|---|---|---|---|---|
| | | | = | |

SCORE /4

**5 You buy some strawberries to share with your brother and sister. There are thirty strawberries. How many do you have each?**

| Number | Sign | Number | | Answer |
|---|---|---|---|---|
| | | | = | |

SCORE /4

Remember – from now on, all you write down is the answer!

TOTAL /20

## TEST 2

✗ or ✔

1. If the stamps for four postcards cost £1.04p, how much did the stamp for each postcard cost?
2. If you share a box of chocolates with five of your friends and you each get four, how many were there in the box?
3. Which is more, three sevens or four fives?
4. Over the last six months there were thirty centimetres of rain. What's the monthly average?
5. Your uncle gives you a ten pound note to share with your brother. What's your share?
6. If pigs had wings, how many wings would twelve pigs have?
7. If you save 50p a month for a year, how much will you have at the end of it?
8. If you have twenty plums to share and there are four of you, how many do you get each?
9. Cat food costs 35p a tin and you need ten tins. How much will it cost?
10. Which is less: five fives or four sixes?

Score 2 points for each correct answer.

TOTAL /20

# «««« Speed training 3 »»»»

## ‹ Speed Test 1 ›

1. 12 – 4 = ☐
2. 3 x 4 = ☐
3. 15 ÷ 3 = ☐
4. 11 – 5 = ☐
5. 6 + 7 = ☐
6. 12 ÷ 4 = ☐
7. 10 ÷ 10 = ☐
8. 13 + 7 = ☐
9. 15 – 6 = ☐
10. 4 x 3 = ☐

**Time** ☐ **seconds**

## ‹ Speed Test 2 ›

1. 7 + 4 = ☐
2. 18 – 9 = ☐
3. 4 x 5 = ☐
4. 10 ÷ 2 = ☐
5. 19 + 1 = ☐
6. 3 x 6 = ☐
7. 12 – 3 = ☐
8. 12 ÷ 3 = ☐
9. 9 x 2 = ☐
10. 8 x 8 = ☐

**Time** ☐ **seconds**

## ‹ Speed Test 3 ›

1. 2 x 7 = ☐
2. 8 + 4 = ☐
3. 14 – 6 = ☐
4. 12 ÷ 2 = ☐
5. 3 x 6 = ☐
6. 7 + 8 = ☐
7. 14 – 7 = ☐
8. 18 ÷ 9 = ☐
9. 7 + 9 = ☐
10. 15 ÷ 5 = ☐

**Time** ☐ **seconds**

## ‹ Speed Test 4 ›

1. 18 ÷ 6 = ☐
2. 9 + 8 = ☐
3. 9 x 2 = ☐
4. 11 – 4 = ☐
5. 4 x 5 = ☐
6. 4 x 4 = ☐
7. 15 ÷ 3 = ☐
8. 8 + 5 = ☐
9. 18 – 9 = ☐
10. 14 – 3 = ☐

**Time** ☐ **seconds**

**Best time with all answers correct**

☐ **seconds**

# Mental arithmetic in real life

## Weight and money

**Bananas**
**£1.10 per kg**

**Pears**
**90p per kg**

**Apples**
**£1.00 per kg**

**Oranges**
**£1.50 per kg**

**Cherries**
**£5.00 per kg**

1. **How much would you pay for $^1/_2$ kg of apples?**
2. **How much would you pay for $1^1/_2$ kg of pears?**
3. **If you buy 1 kg of oranges, how much change do you get from £2.00?**
4. **How much would you pay for 250g of cherries?**
5. **You have £3.00. How many kilograms of apples can you buy?**
6. **If you buy 1 kg of apples and $^1/_2$ kg of pears, how much change will you get from £1.50?**
7. **How many grams of cherries will you get for £1.00?**
8. **How much would you pay for 3 kg of bananas?**
9. **How many kilograms of pears can you buy for £1.80?**
10. **If five of you buy 1 kg of cherries, how much will each of you pay?**

Score 2 points for each correct answer.

**TOTAL** /20

# Estimating money

**Round each price up or down to the nearest £1.**
**For amounts up to 49p: round down.**
**For amounts between 50p and 99p: round up.**

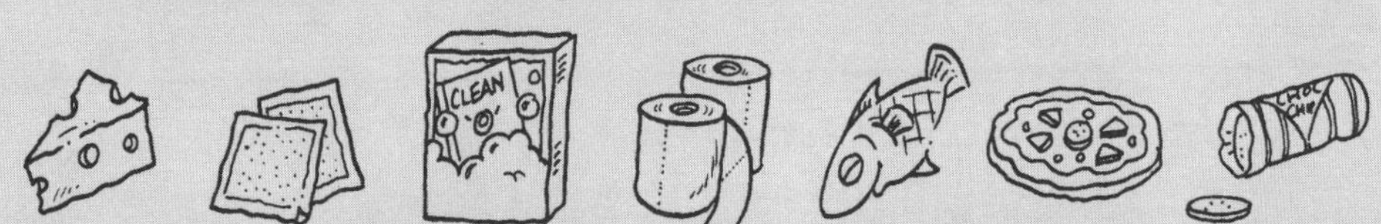

| Cheese | Teabags | Washing powder | Toilet rolls | Fish | Pizza | Biscuits | |
|---|---|---|---|---|---|---|---|
| £3.35 | £1.55 | £2.27 | £2.15 | £4.75 | £2.68 | £2.17 | |
| ↓ | ↓ | ↓ | ↓ | ↓ | ↓ | ↓ | **Estimated total** |

**ROUND UP OR DOWN**

**1** ◯ + ◯ + ◯ + ◯ + ◯ + ◯ + ◯ = ▭

Now work out the exact total with a calculator.

**Exact total**

**2** **£3.35 + £1.55 + £2.27 + £2.15 + £4.75 + £2.68 + £2.17 =** ▭

**3** **How much difference is there between the two totals?**

▭ **difference**

# Estimating area

**You want a new carpet for your bedroom. Your bedroom is 5m 20cm long and 3m 75cm wide.**

**Round up or down to the nearest metre:**

**5m long and 4m wide**

**To find the area in square metres, multiply LENGTH by WIDTH.**

❶ **5m x 4m = 20 m²**

Now do a calculator check.

**5.2m x 3.75m = ______ m²**

**Using the calculator, take the SMALLER number from the BIGGER one.**

❷ ______ **difference**

**Your mum has an old caravan and she wants to carpet the floor. It is 6m 20cm long and 2m 75cm wide.**

If you round up or down to the nearest metre:

1. **How long is it? = ______ m**
2. **How wide is it? = ______ m**
3. **How many square metres is that? = ______ $m^2$**

Now do a calculator check.

4. **6.2m x 2.75m = ______ $m^2$**
5. **What's the difference? = ______ $m^2$**

**There is another way of estimating area.**

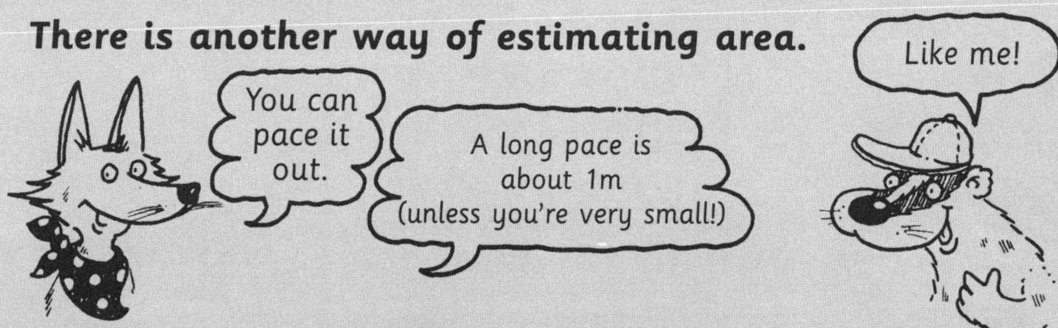


Practise pacing out and estimating area.

# ‹‹‹‹ Speed training 4 ››››

## ‹ Speed Test 1 ›

1. 11 – 9 =
2. 2 x 8 =
3. 7 + 5 =
4. 17 – 8 =
5. 4 x 4 =
6. 20 ÷ 5 =
7. 7 + 7 =
8. 11 – 7 =
9. 11 + 7 =
10. 20 ÷ 2 =

Time ______ seconds

## ‹ Speed Test 2 ›

1. 7 x 2 =
2. 19 – 9 =
3. 6 x 3 =
4. 15 – 8 =
5. 14 ÷ 2 =
6. 2 + 11 =
7. 7 + 9 =
8. 10 ÷ 1 =
9. 17 x 1 =
10. 8 + 8 =

Time ______ seconds

## ‹ Speed Test 3 ›

1. 20 ÷ 5 =
2. 17 – 9 =
3. 4 x 5 =
4. 8 x 2 =
5. 5 + 9 =
6. 4 + 11 =
7. 18 ÷ 2 =
8. 7 x 2 =
9. 18 – 13 =
10. 17 – 17 =

Time ______ seconds

## ‹ Speed Test 4 ›

1. 16 + 1 =
2. 18 – 8 =
3. 16 ÷ 4 =
4. 9 x 2 =
5. 11 – 10 =
6. 5 + 13 =
7. 19 x 1 =
8. 17 ÷ 1 =
9. 13 + 6 =
10. 17 – 15 =

Time ______ seconds

**Best time with all answers correct**

______ seconds

# Time

**Most clocks and watches look like this:**

**This kind of clock is called a dial clock.**

**But some look like this:**
**This kind of clock is called a digital clock, or a 24-hour clock.**

**In the morning (from 24:00 hours to 12:00 hours), both clocks tell the time in the same way:**

**(9:00 a.m.)**

**In the afternoon and evening (from 12:00 to 24:00 hours), the dial clock tells the time like this:**

**(9:00 p.m.)**

**...and the 24-hour clock tells the time like this:**

**(9:00 p.m.)**

**On the 24-hour clock, a p.m. time is an a.m. time + 12 hours:**

1. 15:00 hours = **3.00 p.m.**
2. 23:00 hours = ______
3. 13:00 hours = ______
4. 17:00 hours = ______
5. 20:00 hours = ______
6. 19:00 hours = ______
7. 15:30 hours = **3.30 p.m.**
8. 23:30 hours = ______
9. 13:15 hours = ______
10. 17:15 hours = ______
11. 20:45 hours = ______
12. 19:45 hours = ______

Now try these.

13. 03:00 hours = **3.00 a.m.**
14. 16:00 hours = ______
15. 12:00 hours = ______

16. 07:00 hours = ______
17. 09:30 hours = **9.30 a.m.**
18. 19:30 hours = ______
19. 06:45 hours = ______
20. 22:00 hours = ______
21. 11:30 hours = ______
22. 15:15 hours = ______
23. 24:00 hours = ______
24. 01:10 hours = ______

Score 1 point for each correct answer.

**TOTAL** ___ / 24

1. If your train leaves at 08:30 hours and gets to London at 12:30 hours, how long does the journey take?
2. If your bus leaves at 07:00 hours and gets to town at 07:30 hours, how long does the journey take?
3. If your plane leaves at 18:00 hours and gets to Portugal at 20:30 hours, how long is the flight?
4. If your plane leaves at 12:30 hours and you have to check in two hours before, at what time will you check in?
5. If your train leaves at 23:00 hours and reaches Glasgow at 02:00 hours, how long does the journey take?
6. If your train leaves London at 11:00 hours and the journey takes $1\frac{1}{2}$ hours, at what time do you arrive?
7. If you get to Paris at 13:30 hours by Eurostar after a $3\frac{1}{2}$ hour journey, at what time did you leave?
8. Your bus was due to arrive at 22:30 hours but it is half an hour late. What time does it arrive at the bus station?

**TOTAL** /16

Score 2 points for each correct answer.

# «««« Speed training 5 »»»»

## ❮ Speed Test 1 ❯

| | | |
|---|---|---|
| 1 | 5 + 6 + 4 = | |
| 2 | 3 x 7 = | |
| 3 | 22 – 10 = | |
| 4 | 24 ÷ 6 = | |
| 5 | 11 + 13 = | |
| 6 | 30 ÷ 10 = | |
| 7 | 27 – 8 = | |
| 8 | 7 + 7 + 7 = | |
| 9 | 5 x 6 = | |
| 10 | 30 – 12 = | |

**Time** ☐ **seconds**

## ❮ Speed Test 2 ❯

| | | |
|---|---|---|
| 1 | 29 – 11 = | |
| 2 | 4 x 7 = | |
| 3 | 27 ÷ 9 = | |
| 4 | 8 + 3 + 9 = | |
| 5 | 17 + 7 = | |
| 6 | 24 – 11 = | |
| 7 | 30 ÷ 5 = | |
| 8 | 20 ÷ 1 = | |
| 9 | 9 x 3 = | |
| 10 | 17 + 9 = | |

**Time** ☐ **seconds**

## ❮ Speed Test 3 ❯

| | | |
|---|---|---|
| 1 | 29 – 14 = | |
| 2 | 5 x 7 = | |
| 3 | 8 + 15 = | |
| 4 | 30 ÷ 15 = | |
| 5 | 3 x 9 = | |
| 6 | 26 – 17 = | |
| 7 | 25 ÷ 5 = | |
| 8 | 7 + 8 + 9 = | |
| 9 | 7 x 4 = | |
| 10 | 28 ÷ 2 = | |

**Time** ☐ **seconds**

## ❮ Speed Test 4 ❯

| | | |
|---|---|---|
| 1 | 3 x 8 = | |
| 2 | 27 – 13 = | |
| 3 | 27 ÷ 3 = | |
| 4 | 3 + 11 + 9 = | |
| 5 | 8 x 3 = | |
| 6 | 19 + 7 = | |
| 7 | 21 ÷ 3 = | |
| 8 | 11 x 2 = | |
| 9 | 30 – 18 = | |
| 10 | 22 ÷ 11 = | |

**Time** ☐ **seconds**

**Best time with all answers correct**

☐ **seconds**

# Adding money quickly

**Start with the biggest coin or note.**

**Then add the next biggest one, and then the next biggest one.**

**50p → 70p → 80p → 90p → 95p → 97p → 99p → £1**

**Total**

Now try these.

❶ ☐ → ☐ → ☐ → ☐ → ☐

**Total**

❷ ☐ → ☐ → ☐ → ☐ → ☐ → ☐

**Total**

❸ ☐ → ☐ → ☐ → ☐ → ☐ → ☐

**Total**

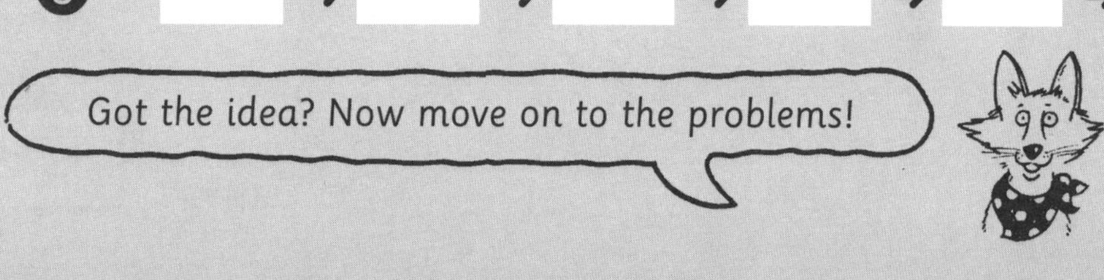

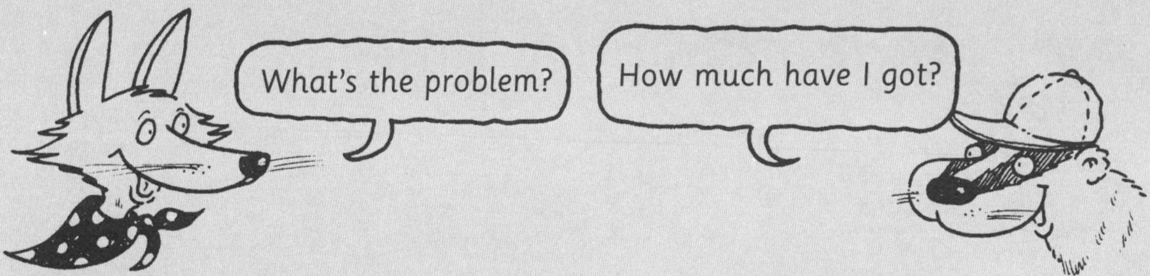


1 

**How much?**

2 

**How much?**

3 

**How much?**

4 

**How much?**

5 

**How much?**

6 **You've got two 50p coins, two 10p coins and three 1p coins. How much?**

7 **You've got two £1 coins, two 20p coins and two 10p coins. How much?**

8 **You've got a £1 coin, two 50p coins, three 10p coins and four 1p coins. How much?**

9 **You've got four £1 coins, two 50p coins, two 20p coins and one 10p coin. How much?**

10 **You've got two £1 coins, two 50p coins, two 20p coins and two 5p coins. How much?**

Score 2 points for each correct answer.

**TOTAL**

/20

# TEST 3

✗ or ✓

1. Add eleven and twelve, and take away three.
2. If you have £10.00 and you spend a quarter of it, how much do you have left?
3. Estimate the total cost of cheese at £2.79, bread at 85p and meat at £4.40.
4. What is half of fifty added to half of forty?
5. Estimate the area of your garage if it is 2m 75cm wide and 6m 15cm long.
6. Which is more: ten sevens or seven tens?
7. What do $1^1/_2$kg of bananas cost at £1.20 per kilogram?
8. You buy some wallpaper for your bedroom at £4.50 per roll. You need six rolls. How much will it cost?
9. Three of you are going camping. The supplies weigh 45kg. How many kilograms will you each have to carry?
10. For three spelling tests you got $^{15}/_{20}$, $^{17}/_{20}$ and $^{18}/_{20}$. How many marks did you lose?

Score 2 points for each correct answer.

TOTAL /20

# ANSWERS

**PAGE 3**

**Speed Test 1** ❶ 3 ❷ 2 ❸ 3 ❹ 1 ❺ 2 ❻ 4 ❼ 2 ❽ 6

**Speed Test 2** ❶ 3 ❷ 8 ❸ 8 ❹ 2 ❺ 10 ❻ 4 ❼ 1 ❽ 10

**Speed Test 3** ❶ 10 ❷ 0 ❸ 3 ❹ 9 ❺ 8 ❻ 10 ❼ 2 ❽ 4

**Speed Test 4** ❶ 6 ❷ 10 ❸ 7 ❹ 10 ❺ 0 ❻ 6 ❼ 10 ❽ 5

**PAGE 4**

❶ 61 ❷ 41 ❸ 62 ❹ 62 ❺ 52 ❻ 71 ❼ 92 ❽ 72 ❾ 92 ❿ 82

**PAGE 5**

❶ 9 ❷ 19 ❸ 39 ❹ 18 ❺ 18 ❻ 11 ❼ 19 ❽ 18 ❾ 18 ❿ 28

**PAGE 7**

❶ £14 + £6 = £20
❷ 17 + 4 = 21 ❸ 28 − 4 = 24
❹ 12 − 10 = 2 ❺ 31p − 15p = 16p

**Page 8 Test 1**

❶ 40p ❷ 10 ❸ 17
❹ 100cm/1m ❺ £1.50 ❻ 8
❼ 31 ❽ 60 ❾ 27kg ❿ 20cm

**PAGE 9**

**Speed Test 1** ❶ 4 ❷ 4 ❸ 10 ❹ 3 ❺ 9 ❻ 1 ❼ 9 ❽ 3

**Speed Test 2** ❶ 10 ❷ 11 ❸ 1 ❹ 0 ❺ 8 ❻ 1 ❼ 1 ❽ 2

**Speed Test 3** ❶ 8 ❷ 7 ❸ 2 ❹ 12 ❺ 15 ❻ 3 ❼ 3 ❽ 0

**Speed Test 4** ❶ 5 ❷ 2 ❸ 9 ❹ 2 ❺ 9 ❻ 1 ❼ 10 ❽ 3

**PAGE 10**

❶ 66 ❷ 60 ❸ 65 ❹ 48 ❺ 48 ❻ 75 ❼ 54 ❽ 84 ❾ 54 ❿ 84

**PAGE 12**

**Table Test 1** ❶ 36 ❷ 21 ❸ 99 ❹ 24 ❺ 72 ❻ 72 ❼ 110 ❽ 42 ❾ 35 ❿ 16

**Table Test 2** ❶ 21 ❷ 100 ❸ 35 ❹ 60 ❺ 24 ❻ 48 ❼ 77 ❽ 144 ❾ 63 ❿ 63

**Table Test 3** ❶ 18 ❷ 90 ❸ 48 ❹ 36 ❺ 28 ❻ 121 ❼ 99 **8** 40 **9** 72 **10** 36

**Table Test 4** ❶ 28 ❷ 64 ❸ 45 ❹ 66 ❺ 132 ❻ 54 ❼ 84 ❽ 72 ❾ 110 ❿ 108

**PAGE 14**

❶ 8 ❷ 4 ❸ 6 ❹ 3 ❺ 4 ❻ 5 ❼ 5 ❽ 3 ❾ 10 ❿ 9 ⓫ 4 r2 ⓬ 5 r1 ⓭ 7 r1 ⓮ 3 r2 ⓯ 7 r1

**PAGE 16**

❶ 180 ❷ 1800 ❸ 1 000
❹ 10 000 ❺ 24 000
❻ 30 000 ❼ 80 000
❽ 2 000 000 ❾ 8 000 000
❿ 90 000 000

**PAGE 17**

❶ £2 x 7 = £14 ❷ 24 ÷ 3 = 8
❸ 6 x 3 = 18 ❹ 6 x 4 = 24
❺ 30 ÷ 3 = 10

**Page 18 Test 2**

❶ 26p ❷ 24 ❸ three sevens
❹ 5cm ❺ £5.00 ❻ 24
❼ £6.00 ❽ 5 ❾ £3.50
❿ four sixes

**PAGE 19**

**Speed Test 1** ❶ 8 ❷ 12 ❸ 5 ❹ 6 ❺ 13 ❻ 3 ❼ 1 ❽ 20 ❾ 9 ❿ 12

**Speed Test 2** ❶ 11 ❷ 9 ❸ 20 ❹ 5 ❺ 20 ❻ 18 ❼ 9 ❽ 4 ❾ 18 ❿ 64

**Speed Test 3** ❶ 14 ❷ 12 ❸ 8 ❹ 6 ❺ 18 ❻ 15 ❼ 7 ❽ 2 ❾ 16 ❿ 3

**Speed Test 4** ❶ 3 ❷ 17 ❸ 18 ❹ 7 ❺ 20 ❻ 16 ❼ 5 ❽ 13 ❾ 9 ❿ 11

**PAGE 20**

❶ 50p ❷ £1.35p ❸ 50p
❹ £1.25 ❺ 3kg ❻ 5p
❼ 200g ❽ £3.30 ❾ 2kg
❿ £1.00

**PAGE 21**

❶ £3 £2 £2 £2 £5 £3 £2 £19
❷ £18.92 ❸ 8p

**PAGE 22**

❶ $19.5m^2$ ❷ $0.5m^2$

**PAGE 23**

❶ 6m ❷ 3m ❸ $18m^2$
❹ $17.05m^2$ ❺ $0.95m^2$

**PAGE 24**

**Speed Test 1** ❶ 2 ❷ 16 ❸ 12 ❹ 9 ❺ 16 ❻ 4 ❼ 14 ❽ 4 ❾ 18 ❿ 10

**Speed Test 2** ❶ 14 ❷ 10 ❸ 18 ❹ 7 ❺ 7 ❻ 13 ❼ 16 ❽ 10 ❾ 17 ❿ 16

**Speed Test 3** ❶ 4 ❷ 8 ❸ 20 ❹ 16 ❺ 14 ❻ 15 ❼ 9 ❽ 14 ❾ 5 ❿ 0

**Speed Test 4** ❶ 17 ❷ 10 ❸ 4 ❹ 18 ❺ 1 ❻ 18 ❼ 19 ❽ 17 ❾ 19 ❿ 2

**PAGE 26**

❶ 3.00 p.m. ❷ 11.00 p.m.
❸ 1.00 p.m. ❹ 5.00 p.m.
❺ 8.00 p.m. ❻ 7.00 p.m.
❼ 3.30 p.m. ❽ 11.30 p.m.
❾ 1.15 p.m. ❿ 5.15 p.m.
⓫ 8.45 p.m. ⓬ 7.45 p.m.
⓭ 3.00 a.m. ⓮ 4.00 p.m.
⓯ 12.00 a.m. ⓰ 7.00 a.m.
⓱ 9.30 a.m. ⓲ 7.30 p.m.
⓳ 6.45 a.m. ⓴ 10.00 p.m.
● 11.30 a.m. ● 3.15 p.m.
● 12.00 p.m. ● 1.10 a.m.

**PAGE 27**

❶ 4 hours ❷ 30 minutes
❸ 2 hours 30 minutes
❹ 10:30 hours ❺ 3 hours
❻ 12:30 hours ❼ 10:00 hours
❽ 23:00 hours

**PAGE 28**

**Speed Test 1** ❶ 15 ❷ 21 ❸ 12 ❹ 4 ❺ 24 ❻ 3 ❼ 19 ❽ 21 ❾ 30 ❿ 18

**Speed Test 2** ❶ 18 ❷ 28 ❸ 3 ❹ 20 ❺ 24 ❻ 13 ❼ 6 ❽ 20 ❾ 27 ❿ 26

**Speed Test 3** ❶ 15 ❷ 35 ❸ 23 ❹ 2 ❺ 27 ❻ 9 ❼ 5 ❽ 24 ❾ 28 ❿ 14

**Speed Test 4** ❶ 24 ❷ 14 ❸ 9 ❹ 23 ❺ 24 ❻ 26 ❼ 7 ❽ 22 ❾ 12 ❿ 2

**PAGE 29**

❶ 50p 60p 65p 67p 68p
❷ £1 £1.50 £1.60 £1.65 £1.67 £1.68
❸ 50p £1.00 £1.20 £1.30 £1.32 £1.34

**PAGE 30**

❶ £2.70 ❷ £1.55 ❸ £1.54
❹ 95p ❺ £2.00 ❻ £1.23
❼ £2.60 ❽ £2.34 ❾ £5.50
❿ £3.50

**Page 31 Test 3**

❶ 20 ❷ £7.50 ❸ £8.00
❹ 45 ❺ $18m^2$
❻ They are the same ❼ £1.80
❽ £27.00 ❾ 15kg ❿ 10